Literature written for young adults...

by young adults.

Allow yourself to be surprised.

Phases

Young Writers Chapbook Series

Elizabeth Garnes

Atlanta

Copyright © 2013 by Elizabeth Garnes
Published by VerbalEyze Press

All rights reserved. Printed in the United States of America. No part of this book may be used or reproduced in any manner whatsoever, including Internet usage, without written permission from VerbalEyze Press except in the case of brief quotations embodied in critical articles and reviews.

Cover design by Kerany Koehl
Editing by Derek Koehl and Tavares Stephens
ISBN: 978-0-9856451-3-7

VerbalEyze Press books are available at special discounts for bulk purchases in the United States by corporations, institutions and other organizations.

For information, address VerbalEyze Press, 1376 Fairbanks Street SW, Atlanta, Georgia 30310.

VerbalEyze does not participate, endorse, or have any authority or responsibility concerning private correspondence between our authors and the public. All mail addressed to authors are forwarded, but the publisher cannot, unless specifically instructed by the author, give out an address or phone number.

VerbalEyze Press
A division of VerbalEyze, Inc.
www.verbaleyze.org

Table of Contents

Foreword 11
Editors' Note 13
Memories 15
Air 17
Rosemary 19
Water.. 21
Ink 23
Phases of Faces 25
Sweet and Sour 27
Truth 29
Never.. 31
13 Ways to Look at the Moon.. 33

Phases

Foreword

Many a black and white speckled notebook has been privy to the growing pains of young artists. They sketch, narrate, poet and rhyme to make sense of the world and orient themselves to the gravitational pull of coming of age. But their musings beg for answers and an empathetic head nod, so YaHeard? Poetics was born.

Whether speaking heartache at the mic, spitting social commentary over tracks or texting observations into the ether, the power and influence of word is undeniable and YaHeard? Poets study the craft, explore their creative process and learn how to promote their artistic endeavors through collaborations with organizations like VerbalEyze, a beacon for young artists.

YaHeard? was founded by Educator-Artists to support the creative stirrings of tweens and teens and the publication of this chapbook honors and encourages the work of a young artists whose passion and talent confirms them as part of a new generation of prolific writers, artists and musicians. Their musings have escaped from first notebooks and into your hands. Answer if you dare; head nod if you must ---this young scribe dares to explore the power of voice.

Ya Heard?

Susan Arauz Barnes
Co-founder, YaHeard? Poetics

Editors' Note

The Young Writers Chapbook Series is an expression of the mission and vision that is core to what we do at VerbalEyze. Through this series, we are able to provide talented, emerging young authors their debut introduction to the reading public. We are grateful that you also share an enthusiasm for young authors and the vibrant and energized perspectives they bring to our shared understanding of the human experience and what it means to live, love, long, lose and wonder as we travel together through this world.

We are pleased to bring to you an exceptional young writer, Elizabeth Garnes, with this edition of the Young Writers Chapbook. We trust that you will be as engaged and challenged by her words as we have been. Elizabeth is part of an exceptional group of young writers, YaHeard? Poetics. She and her fellow writers are an never-ending encouragement and inspiration to us.

Read, enjoy and, as always, *allow yourself to be surprised*.

Derek Koehl
Tavares Stephens

Memories

Mmmmmm…….

Milestones make miles

Memory

Mindless and

Madness

Moving while

Making

Missing and

Mocking

Memorable Missions

Air

We breathe then forget

One lifetime with each second

We value nothing

Rosemary

Sweet without notice

In every second of life

Love without knowledge

Water

Calm and soothing waves

Bouncing and turning in breeze

Keep a steady beat

Ink

Black

Blue

Red

Colors of the world
Squeezed in a lifeless tube
Disintegrates against paper
Forming words and thoughts
Making a new place
For

A new idea

A new start

A new soul

Phases of Faces

Sweet face

Nice face

Mean face

Ugly face

Funny face

But where is the real face?

Oh, right

It is hidden

Under all the fake ones

Sweet and Sour

Sweet Side

Nice

Truthful

Meaningful

Fake

Sour Side

Mean

Hateful

Rude

Fake

Creative Side

True

Wild

Original

Real

Truth

Would you like to know the truth?

You will never be good enough

It's never enough

You're always judged

Teased and ridiculed

Once upon a time

That never happened

A better time

A time beyond imagining

Never

Never will I say never

Unless its forever

Saying never forever

Is saying forever never

Not as clever

As no forever

As in never

13 Ways to Look at the Moon

I
Takes
The sun's spotlight

II
Phases
Like different faces

III
It is day
At night

IV
It shimmers
Like the inside
Of an eye
The opening to
The soul

V
Nothing equals
This brightness

VI
12 hours
Of emptiness

VII
The night sky's
Only companion

VIII
Inside
And out
It twinkles

IX
White as snow
Waiting for
Discovery

X
Magnifying
Its own mysteries

XI
Milestone
in the making

XII
Like white snowflakes
Of a snowball

XIII
The night's
Center
of attention

Elizabeth Garnes is a poet, artist and performer. Elizabeth has been writing poetry since the age of 10 and that is when she discovered her love for it. She discovered this love in 6th grade during the poetry unit. She realized that she expressed her feelings in writing better than any other way. Since then, Elizabeth has been working to improve her talent, continuing to explore her passion for poetry.

She currently lives in Atlanta, GA.

Photo credit: Tammy Garnes

Empowering young writers to say, **"I am my scholarship!"**

Open call for submissions to the *Young Writers Anthology*!

See your work in print!

        Become a published writer!

                Earn royalites that can help you pay for college!s

VerbalEyze Press is accepting submissions from young adult writers, ages 13 to 22, in any of the following genres:

- poetry
- short story
- songwriting
- playwriting
- graphic novel
- creative non-fiction

For submission details, visit
www.verbaleyze.org

VerbalEyze serves to foster, promote and support the development and professional growth of emerging young writers.

VerbalEyze is a nonprofit organization whose mission is to foster, promote and support the development and professional growth of emerging young writers.

The *Young Writers Anthology* is published as a service of VerbalEyze in furtherance of its goal to provide young writers with access to publishing opportunities that they otherwise would not have.

Fifty percent of the proceeds received from the sale of the *Young Writers Anthology* are paid to the authors in the form of scholarships to help them advance in their post-secondary education.

For more information about VerbalEyze and how you can become involved in its work with young writers, visit www.verbaleyze.org.

www.ingramcontent.com/pod-product-compliance
Lightning Source LLC
Chambersburg PA
CBHW032106040426
42449CB00007B/1206